CW01467067

Once again I would like to thank the following people for their support: Claire Curran, Claire McKeown, Margaret Walker, Darren Livingstone and all at Sink The Ink, Emily and Matthew Harris.

I would also like to thank Tina and all at Excalibur Press for all their hard work and for giving me the opportunity to have my work in print xx.

"Maybe We Are All Members Of An Orchestra That Is Merely Tuning Up And Our Curious Trails Are Random Scales For A Music That Has Yet To Begin".......Tom Waits

"All Systems You Contrive Without Us, Will Be Brought Down".........Leonard Cohen

The contents and views of this book do not have anything to do with the publisher but lie in my head of beliefs and ideals....
...Mark Evison

CONTENTS

THUMP

The mumbling voices from the TV flood through the wall

THUMP! THUMP! THUMP in my head

Voices getting louder

6am Sunday Morning, Christ on a bike

What in the fuck is she watching?

The kitchen awaits with a welcome glass of cool water

My hangover fries my brain

The coolness of the water drowns my arid tonsils but like

every hangover known to us my throat is soon like sandpaper

Will she ever turn that fucker off?

My mind tunes into the distortion

Will It ever stop?

PLEASE!

Sleep along with Elvis has left the building

Jesus, she's only gone and turned the fucker up

6.30am on a Sunday Morning may well be the last time she

breathes

THUMP! THUMP! THUMP!

TEA & TOAST

Tea and Toast with Raspberry jam

Not with Ham or Spam

Just seedy raspberry jam

Tea, two sugars and a little milk

AAAHHH, That's lovely, That's my ilk

Cheese on toast adored by most

But for me

It's raspberry jam upon my toast.

For "Big Flynn and Gerry Dorby"

CHRIST

Christ, Will someone turn that fucking alarm off

Christ, I'm the only one here

Christ, It's 6am

Christ, I'm hungover

Christ, I've got breakfasts this morning

Christ, It's 9am

Christ, I've still a hangover

Christ, I'm late

Christ, Who in the fuck is knocking on my door

Christ, It's the fucking boss

Christ, Christ, Christ.

LAZY AUTUMN DAYS

The day has dragged by

Listening to the sound of the brook out back

Whistling wind makes music with the swaying trees

Leaves fall to the sodden ground

Skeletons of Summer are left behind

Winter will be here soon

For now though, Autumn is fighting a losing battle

Mist crawls over the Belfast Hills

Soon to smother the view in its white shroud

Rain pelts the double glazing

It's cosy to be inside

Snuggling up on the couch

The Sandman soon comes a calling

Bringing dreams of lazy Autumn days

SOLITAIRE

When you're alone,

Where do you go

Solitary constraints of your mind

Playing tricks, unpleasant and unkind

"When you're alone and you are lonely

Then you're in trouble"

I heard that once

Doubt if there's a truer quote

If so I've yet to find

As I slowly but surely go out of my mind

CHRISTY

The Christ sings about the Barrowlands

I sit back and smile with a smug grin

PSSSSHHHH goes the tin as I open another

Watching the creamy storm settle into the black of night

My mouth begins to salivate

The frothy top looks like discoloured cream

I lift the pint, I lift my top lip

Let the black liquid oil my throat

As I take a sup

I'm tempted to let out an AAAHHH

Christy interrupts this train of thought

As he sings of an Ireland that once was

Gipsy's, Banshees, Glimmering Trout and the finest of horses

A strange kind of day it's been

The cool liquid washes the melancholy away

I lie back on the couch and listen

Christy sings "Ride On"

And life washes It's sins off my back

Dug

Off the leash and off he runs
Like a Greyhound out of the traps
Nose to the ground sniffing for a trail
Down the wooded lane, barking at Squirrels
Standing on hind legs, front paws on the old Oak
He yelps, barks and waggles his tail at wee grey squirrel ten
feet high
Squeaks sound like laughter as he teases Dug
The hand reaches down, puts him on the leash
Crossing the road obediently, doesn't pay to misbehave with
all those muddy fields awaiting
He knows the fun is about to begin
The hand unclips the lead and off he runs
Once down the auld dirt track, lush green fields are his
playground
He disappears into the thick Bracken
Looking for birds, rabbits and his old friends the Squirrels
Hearing a whistle from afar he digs his way out of the Thicket
He hears the whistle once more and off he flies towards that
direction
His mouth open, Tongue to the side, Ears pinned back
Running like the wind past the whistler and on into the
distance
Picking up a scent he dashes for the trees
Cocking his leg for a quick whizz

The whistle goes up once more and of he runs
Suddenly he turns, runs past his two legged friend
There it is, his oasis and his pals worst nightmare
His tail waggles as he jumps in and lays down in the muddy
puddle, taking drinks of the mucky water
No black and white coat now
The hand clips him back on the lead
Cross the road and back to the auld Oak
No Squirrel this time
A quick sniff, A quick whizz and back up the lane
Almost home for some well deserved water and a chew on his
bone
The Whistler sits down with his cuppa
Dug jumps up on the couch and lays his head on his two
legged friends lap
He snuggles down
The only sound, panting his self into sleep
Dreams of Squirrels, Rabbits and muddy puddles
The coal fire warms the room and soon both Dug and
Whistler are fast asleep

NEEDLESS SLAUGHTER

The girl stands in the street, shock etched into her pretty face
Chaos ensues all around
Anti Terrorist Police, Fire Engines, Ambulances, Sirens,
Screams and smoke fill the night air
It's like watching a disaster movie on mute
A high pitched buzzing fills her head
A Gendame pulls his gun as he walks towards her
He shouts at her, The buzzing and noises of horror are too
intense inside her head for her to hear
Aiming the gun at her with one hand, signalling with the other
for her to fall on bended knee
This can't be happening
Dazed, Confused, She thinks for a fleeting a moment did I do
this, No of course not
Her fiancée pushed her out the way, His reward to be blown
all over the building
His blood and guts cover her
The Gendame shouts again
She snaps from her confusion into the ensuing horror
Moroccan Woman, Dark skin, Muslim, Guilty till proven
innocent
This can't be happening
"SHOOT!" She screams
"I want to be with my love" she pleads
Blood from her head fills her eyes

15

The blood stings, She wipes it away only for it to return
seconds later
Suddenly she collapses to the ground
The Gendame is confused, He of course is sadly wrong
A Paramedic comes to her rescue, An Ambulance rushes her
away
She did not die today, She did not join the list of many
A new life for her as mental scars, Mental health, Images of a
lost love will all demand a small piece of her on a daily basis
All they wanted was to celebrate their love
To shout and scream in wild abandonment to the sounds of
Bataclan
Sneak a kiss, Sneak loving glances
Instead slaughter of 127
In the name of Allah, In the name of Christ
This is what religion does
There is nothing Islamic or Christian about needless slaughter
There is nothing left but the death of innocence.

WINTER IS A COMING

Walking into the wooded Glen darkened skies open
Rain pelts down
Pattering of rain on the last of Autumn leaves
The babbling brook flows fast and furious
Lifting the dirt from the bed, The swirling torrent leaves a
creamy soapy scum on top
Could be mistaken for a pint with that frothy top
Trees reach tall into the sky
Clambering up, Branches stretched out, reaching for the last
rays of sunlight
The ground is thick with sodden brown leaves
Mother Earths carpet
Sounds of rushing water get louder
Standing on the bridge, looking down, The waterfall cascades
into the flowing brook
Water rushes away saying goodbye as it takes its long trip
seaward bound
A dog soaked and muddy runs towards its owner
A week or two now and the trees will be skeletons of winter
Animals will hibernate
Only the babbling brook will be heard
The wee chirping Robin looking for winter fruits
A wee reminder that in fact Winter is a coming.

Family Honour

Seventeen and on the run
Her family have hired someone
Someone to care for their family honour
She fell in love with a Punjab
He fell in love with her sex
Left her with child
Disgust, Shame, How will the family hold its honour
Can't have news reaching Pakistan, They will fall from grace
No wives or dowries for the eldest son
No riches will adorn their pathetic door
If the man had been Urdhu then maybe....
How could she? How could she bring such shame?
Fleeing from friends, Fleeing from so called family
Sleeping on the streets, Another homeless statistic
Every sound keeps her awake
No money, No place to go, No hope
The family hunt for her life
She hunts for her freedom
A shelter for abused women is her refuge
Finding her a new home, A new town, A new identity
She will have her baby
She will be safe
Her daughter will grow into a beautiful woman
No religious values in this household
Sadly thousands of young women will not be so lucky
May their god have mercy on their souls and show no mercy
to those of family honour.

A MISSED LOVE

The stillness of the room is alive with his sadness

Distant sounds of passing traffic

Brings memories of when you left

Your smell hangs in the air like a city smog

Pain stabs at me every day

" Memories in the corners of my mind...."

Sang Barbra once upon a lifetime ago

Your smile, Your laugh, Your anger, Your kindness, Your

love

Haunt my lonely mind

I long for your touch once more

To hold your hand as we walk along the stormy shoreline

Now like the tides it's gone, forever lost in the winds of time

".....Can be beautiful and yet......"

THE HURLY

Players line up in the pouring rain
Ankles deep in mud
The ball spun into the air
One player jumps higher than the other
Like a Salmon working its way up a waterfall
Patting the ball to a waiting team mate
As the ball flies off the hurly
Rising, soaring through the air
Is it a bird, Is it a plane
Nah,ye fecking eejits It's a hurly ball
Fifty, sixty yards it travels into the forwards hands
Bouncing it off his bat
He runs and jinks past the defenders
Suddenly a thunderous crack silences the crowd
Writhing in agony, The forward is unaware of the ensuing
battle
Bats break or are thrown to the ground
Fists fly, A nose breaks, A skull splits open
Eventually it will simmer down
The game will resume
Gaelic myths and legends summoned the Celtic warriors to
take part in days of yore
Now played by mere mortals
This game of ours
A gift from The Gods of War
But for all who play
A Celtic Warrior is born.

The Coffee Shop

As you walk to your table the clinking of cutlery greets you
like nattering Gulls on the seashore
Smells of home baked goods give your tummy a belly rumble
Wood on wood as you scrape your chair out along the floor
Sitting down you scrape the chair back into place
The waitress gives you a minute
Settled, Good, Now what's that order
Puch, puch, puchs of the coffee machine fill the air as it
jumps into cappuccino mode
Frothy milk wi' a wee drop of the brown nectar
A sprinkle of chocolate or cinnamon and away ye go
KGB whispers can be heard from the blue rinse brigade in the
corner
Everyone a Stalin in their own living room
Complaining about the youth of today
Answer me this oh Granny Stalin
Who set the standards for the youth of today
Are they not passed from generation to generation
Cappuccino heaven arrives with two packs of brown sugar
and a wee tottie biscuit

21

Very swish, very suave, very fucking expensive

Slurping the coffee upsets the blue rinse brigade into wild

hysteria

Cackling like hyenas at a carcass on the Serengeti Plains

You don't care, Why would you

As the coffee is slurped to its conclusion

A scraping of the chair once more just to annoy

Pay, leave a tip for the bonnie wee waitress, then out the door

Oh Stalingrad, Oh Stalingrad no more.

Look Cool

£1200 for a new suit

£20 for a new pork pie hat

£150 for nice new shiny shoes

£120 for new Raybans

£100 for a crisp white shirt

£30 for Woolen Socks

£50 for CK kacks

£80 for a trendy haircut and neat trimmed beard

Three minutes off your life for a cigarette

Expensive to look cool.

Lies, Lies, Lies

Who do you think you are?
Manipulate the media the world over
Right wing drivel at someone's expense
It's about abuse of power you openly admit in your defence
Kept quiet about Savile and Rolf
Friends of yours were they? Did you play golf
Still you manipulate with your fascist ideals
" I own the press, I own the TV
I'll make people love me "
You're a disgrace to journalism
Lies, Lies, Lies have you no kinder vision
Citizens of Liverpool have you sussed as you attacked their
fallen in death
What the fuck? Were you on Crystal Meth?
Stop at nothing for a quick buck
It's time for you tae get tae fuck
Sitting in your Ivory Tower
Licking the holes of the right wing in power
You'll be found out when you meet your maker
Then you'll know what's it all about when you're no longer
the taker
Keep taking that Crystal Meth
For remember this we are all equal in death
Lies, Lies, Lies.

CAMOUFLAGE SKIN

The scaly green lizard walks along the fence

Stops every three steps or so, a quick glance then on

His bright leathery skin shines in the early morning sun

It seems like an age for him to get thus far

Suddenly he picks up speed

Leaps of the fence

Lands about a foot away on the bark of a welcome Palm Tree

Red flowers blossom all around

The Lizard safe in the knowledge of camouflage

Where is he?

Wind rustles the branches like a timpani of cymbals

Water in the pool ripples

Water in the canal ripples

In the hot morning sun the Eddie Izzard falls asleep

Safe in his suit of camouflage skin.

THE MILL AND THE DAISY

Walking up the chalky trail
There stands an old rusting Chalk Mill
Outhouses crumble with age under the weight of overrun
branches and Ivy
Mother Nature engulfs Industrialism
All forms of nature rage their revenge on the auld mill
Standing proud in the soft sodden earth are Wild Daisies
One in particular seems more resplendent and proud
Toothpaste white petals cling to the warmth of the summer
sun
Yellow pin cushion like centre
Clouds darken above
Flowers seem to wilt
Animals dart into the growth
But not this Daisy, It dares the clouds to open
They pass over without causing a scene
Fields once again come alive with wildlife
This once proud Mill that gave work to so many is dying and
rusting away
It can die proud as it gives life to Mother Nature's lifeline
Stand tall you proud auld Mill and Resplendent Daisy

MOVING ON WITH HOPE

Sitting on a rocking chair
Gently swaying back and fro
Springsteen singing about better days
Pretty apt what with all the political strife
Yet I have never been so happy with my life
Dark dark days left behind
Family, Dug, Friends all gone
Here I sit on a balcony in a foreign land
A new life to begin with new hope
This time last year who would've thought
In the words of Mr. Bragg "I took the great leap forwards"
A new feeling of excitement inside
An emotion I never had
Nothing to lose I stepped off the edge
Surprise surprise I did not fall
Baby steps is all it takes
When you're moving on with Hope..

THE SNOWY NIGHT

The blizzard has finally ended
Darkness, Brightened by the Moon reflecting off the snowy
ground
Why after snowfall is all left peaceful and calm
Bringing a serenity and freshness to the cold air
Crunching of boots on virgin snow
An auld ruin of a house plays shelter to the creatures of the
forest
Broken glass in cracked window panes
No door where there once was one
It would have kept night like these at bay
Irony is lost on no one
The chimney still stands
In the girth a nest of Robins
A sly old fox creeps in without invitation
Sniffing around, looking for a whiff of a meal
Any scent has been covered by the freshly fallen snow
He disappears, his soft paws make very little sound
Nothing else stirs
Stars sparkle like someone has thrown gold glitter over the
universe
Crossing the sky, A shooting star
Eventually It will burn and fade
Snowy clouds move in and smother the clear moon
Stars have been hoovered up
Snow falls once more
Snowflakes land gently to become the virgin snow.

Summer Of '69

The Stags head looks down on me
Dust accumulates on the antlers
What a terrible waste for such a magnificent beast
Thin Lizzy's version of Whisky In The Jar blasts from
untuned speakers
In competition, The Racing channel blurts out its commentary
Retired men stand and shout as their pensions disappear
A tinged sadness fills the air
These once proud men worked all their lives
Put out to pasture, No worth to industry anymore
Slot machines line various walls
The atmosphere, sullen and dank
No idle chit chat in here
An ignoramace of a barman can't muster the strength to speak
Listens, pours and sticks his hand out
"Please Sir can I have some more" comes to mind
No please, no thanks, no nothing
Locals stare, No hidden glances here
You stare back
Heads swivel as the TV shouts another conclusion to a race
Rotating necks, Robot like, Could be a winner or not
Bryan fae back in the day sings Summer Of '69
Christ!
If only it was Bryan, If only it was
Seems more like a funeral parlour than a local on an afternoon
I finish my pint, Starting to leave, a parting sigh beats me to it
"Back In The Summer Of '69......"

5000% Profit

I know someone lying up there dying, On that ward

Patients down here filling their lungs with tar

Man they ain't even trying

Like the radiation poisoning isn't enough

Idiots down here I guess just ain't that tough

It's okay 'cause Nicotine is Government approved

Can't have Cannabis Oil,

Not FSD approved

You can lose your hair, your teeth and your will to live

They'll line their ever deepened pockets, take all you can give

It's not about a cure for cancer, Not about Cannabis Oil

It's about the fucking profits of which It would spoil

Cancer is big business and that unfortunately is a fact

That man laying up there dying

Fuck the chemical companies they ain't even trying

Isn't enough that Chemo takes your dignity

Don't look to any government they only have excuses not pity

Soon he will be buried, they took everything he had

5000% Profit now that ain't too bad!

THE PICTURE

I sit, stare and ponder over your picture

Sun glasses perched upon your head

A whisper of hair reaches down gently touching the soft skin

of your face

Those hazel eyes maybe dark but they can light up ant room

Your infectious smile

Cheeky wee dimples

Pangs of love stab at my aching heart

It may sound like sadness

I can promise you my love it is not

This picture I kiss every night

It lights up my life

It lights up my day

It lights up the path I must travel to be in your arms

This picture of you by my side

You have lit up my life in a period of darkness

That light has guided me towards you

Learning to love again

Life, love led to happiness

Happiness led me to you

And all the while

This picture I kiss every night

It lights up my day

It lights up my life

This picture of you by my side

The day I pass I will close my eyes

Remembering the love we have

With my last breath I will whisper the words I love you

This picture I kiss for the last time

This picture that has lit up my life

This picture that has lit up my path

This picture that will be buried by my side

No' For Me

Facebook, That book, This book
Whatever happened to the Jungle Book
www.com, Rom com, Sit com
Someone drop a bomb
Twitter, Instagram, Pintrest, This trest
Twaddle, Nae fucking interest
Lap top, Desk top, Table top
Jesus H Christ the world has lost the plot
Messenger, Web cam, Skyping, Texting
Whatever happened to letter writing
Google this and Google that
Open a book and read you twat
Yahoo, Viber, Spotify, PayPal, YouTube
Gie's a brek, You're a tube
The digital age is upon us now
English language take a bow
Words replaced by abbreviation
God help the younger generation
Give me a time when the phone sat in the hall
Give me a time when you were not in to take a call
This digital age is not what it's cracked up to be
This digital age is No' for me

ARMAGEDDON

The light is grey like my unsettled mind

Driving myself into a state of depression

Ah the complexities of the human brain

It's capabilities to do so much good

The capability to do so wrong

Like a flick of a coin on a runaway train

Fate decides who is to gain

Them who have everything keep through greed and
manipulation

Most of the World's population suffer at their hands

Pain, Famine, The rotten stench of desperation

Our planet has to survive

Progress has to survive more no matter the cost

The wealthy pay for progression

Destroy, destroy, destroy like an obsession

Their greed has become their obesity

They hide behind the Churches in the name of Christianity

Collection boxes filled to the brim by the poor given to the
rich

Corrupt Politicians, Corrupt Governments, Corrupt Elections

They hide behind the word terrorism

Islam is bad, Muslim is evil

Sure it must be true, It's on Murdoch's television

They have a vision, They have a mission

Pockets lined with gold on the road to destruction

Greed blinds them

Nuclear weapons will destroy them

They will destroy us

Weapons of mass destruction it's in the name

Armageddon outta here

We won't be back!

WET

Rivulets of water run down the muddy hillside
It could be mistaken for the end of the world
Even the lush green hills look as if they have been put
through a hot wash
Devoid of any colour
No one out walking today
Birds hiding, Drookit in their nests
Sheltered in the thickets doesn't help either
Feathers so heavy, flying is futile
Busy roads are light of traffic today
An unfortunate pedestrian caught in the downpour
Suddenly has an unexpected shower
Drenched in filthy water
A white van driver speeds off laughing at the misfortune he
has caused
"YA FUCKER!!" echoes round the streets
More expletives light up the air
It's the only colour that will happen today
As Randy once sang "Feels like it's raining all over the world"

A Winter's Night

The light outside is dull and dim

Winter darkness creeps in

Bringing an Arctic chill to the night air

Blinds pulled, Curtains drawn

The lamplight gives a shaded warmth to the room

A glass of Whisky sits on the table

The clinking of Ice cubes as they slide and melt their way

round the glass

Robert Wyatt sings Louie's What A Wonderful World

Creamy Saxophone fills the air

Like the Ice, The thoughts of Winter melt

Snapping, crackling, even the odd pop

Goes the wood and coal

Impersonating a Rice Krispie bowl

Flickering away the chill of a Winter's Night

Ocean Sunset

I look out to sea
On the horizon sits a yacht
Water like ice makes the boat seem motionless
No breeze to move it on
The sun is setting
Leaving the yacht alone, soon to be engulfed in darkness
For now oranges, reds, yellows paint up the sky
The ice like sea painted different shades of purple
The Horizon is awash with colour
Looks like a pyromaniac's wet dream
Rivulets in the sand turn golden
Stranded jellyfish pray for the sea to return soon
To come back and forgive them their sins
Wash them on their way to another journey
A slight breeze lets the various seabirds glide across the
current
It sends a wee chill down the spine
Time to go
Time for the tide to drift lazily in taking it's time
Tomorrow will be busy
Beyond the horizon storms are getting ready
Ready to gatecrash the party
Ocean Sunset no more but for now
Sit back, take a sip of your wine and enjoy the view

BIG BRO

No one to listen
Your demons falling on deaf ears
Suicide, Depression, Anxiety, the whole gang come calling
Where can you go without the pressures of Judgement
Instead of falling
Our name is Big Bro
We're here to listen or not
Come Sketch, Learn Music, Learn Poetry
Learn what you want
No such word as can't
We're not here to make you abide
Chill and listen to music
Drink a coffee, you can do that too
Don't be scared to get in touch
We even have a Facebook page
Remember this that you're not alone
And there will always be someone to help you along......

Dedicated to Big Bro, It was the right idea, The right place, Just the wrong time for me but to all who helped and to Darren for pushing it on. This is also for all the people who sometimes just feel a little bit lost.

THE SOLITARY TRUMPET

Creeping over the hills silently
The sky turns charcoal grey
Suddenly like a David Blaine illusion there are no hills
Like an Apache stalking Buffalo
Calmly, quietly, unforgiving
Rain clouds kill Summer
The so called Heavens open
As torrents of water fall from above
Within minutes hilly streets run with streams of dirty water
Leaving a lake like puddle at the bottom
Insufficient drainage systems help the water to leave it's mark
They can't cope, There's only so much water a blocked drain
can handle
All is still
An odd car splashes it's way to journeys end
Rain pattering off rooftops
In the distance a solitary Trumpet plays Miles Kinda Blue
It somehow fits the beat of the rain
The sound sneaks it's way out of the double glazed prison that
this summer weather has us trapped in
The beat is melancholic, hypnotic, Lazy
The Melody settles over Tinsel Town in the rain..

OUTSIDE IS AMERICA

Across the railtracks, past the crack houses
Wandering over Federal
The World hasn't woken, Round here the World hasn't slept
No Sandman here
There past the auld furniture store stands a door
Not like any other door
It leads into a building with no light, no windows, no outside
light here
The door looks lost
We knock, Old Toothless lets us in
Smells of rancid piss
Bee like stings nip your eyes
Bile rises in the throat
Keep it down, No place for weakness in here
Only two white dudes, Fuck
Sticking out like the last two virgin white candles in Chapel
"Two Buds" is the grunt
"Sure Whitey" chuckles the barman enjoying the uncomfort
of it all
Education for the white man he thinks
Two dollars is two dollars
His breath would melt your eyebrows
A CRASH! A poor junkie falls over a table
Crack pipe in hand, stoned into another being
"Throw that Nigga' out, We ain't that kinda place

41

Oh sweet baby irony if you could see this now
People asleep on tables
Someone in the corner is wet
Steam rises and fills the air with Eau de Toilette
No one cares
An unfortunate picks at a gangrenous scab unaware of the
danger
The dregs at the bottom of the World
Stare at the dregs at the bottom of a glass
The smell, Jesus the smell
Time to leave
No work, No healthcare, No housing, No Hope
Outside is middle class U.S fucking A
Floridian sun blinds the unadjusted eyes
As the cries of Donald Frump ring out
"God bless Middle Class America"
God help the rest of them.

THE MEET

I step into Arrivals

Tired and weary

Looking around I catch your eye

"There she Is"

Your smile cleanses my tiredness

Dropping my bags you skip into my arms

I swing you round, hugging you tightly

We stand in front of each other not quite sure what to do next

My heart beats like a John Bonham drum solo

Raising my hand to your blushing cheek

I lean in, Kiss those soft lips

Just long enough to let Bonzo finish off his solo

We smile coyly

We laugh nervously

You take my hand

We wander off into the stifling heat of Lauderdale

Together at last

A Note From The Author

Sorry there is very little correct grammar, spelling etc but I felt something would be lost in the character of the poems. All were written in an extremely difficult period of my life, apart from a name change on one of the poems.

The two volumes of poetry that I have now completed will be my last for a bit as I am currently working on my Journals "The Journal Of A Selfish Bastard" and a book of short stories aptly called "Wee Shorties". I have enclosed a clip from that book. It should be out round Summer '17.

Once again I would like to thank all who have purchased HOPE.

Oh and a wee warning the wee shortie is a wee bit politically incorrect so please don't be offended.

THE CONVERSATION

1/ "Whit in the name of fuck is that smell?"

2/ "Yon big bastard o'er there"

1/ "He's three rows up, no way Jose"

2/ "I'm tellin' you man"

1/ "Awa' and shite"

2/ "Listen when I went for a pish, on the way back I just happened tae follow the smell, I mean Christ on a bike ya cannae miss it. Anyway there he was sweat under the oaxters like a fucking Olympic swimming pool!"

1/ "Ach away yer winding me up"

2/ "I'm no, Right away for a pish and get a wee swatch on the way back"

1/ "Naw 'cause I'll stare"

2/ "Stare! I'd be mair worried ya jump in for a swim"

1/ "Ha,ha,ha ya daft bastard"

2/ "It's no really funny but"

1/ "I'll ask the flying waitress tae give him a bar of soap will I?"

2/ "Imagine the poor James Hunt sitting next tae him. Nae wonder he's asleep, that reek wid knock out a horse"

1/ "Here change the subject, yer gie'ing me the boak"

2/ "Awright well, Did you see yon daft bastard wi' the turban on back at airport security?"

1/ "Naw"

2/ "Whit? Ye must have"

1/ "I'm telling ye I never seen him. Whit? Was it Tony Singh?"

2/ "Who? Whit? Tony who?"

1/ "Singh, The TV Chef"

2/ "Naw! Whit in the name o' fuck?"

1/ "Disnae matter I never seen him"

2/ "BAWS!"

1/ "Baws whit? I never seen him I'm tellin' ye. I wish it was Tony Singh I love his cooking show"

2/ "Will you shut the fuck up about Tony Singh? Are ye gonna let me tell you what happened?"

1/ "Aye, sorry on ye go then"

2/ "Jesus, Tony Singh! Anyway the silly bastard puts his hand luggage through the security screen, next thing he's pulled over"

1/ "Racist bastards, 'cause he had a turban oan?"

2/ "Naw, The silly bastard had all these tools in his bag, A drill, A hammer and a load of other shit. The fucker must have shares in Black and Decker"

1/ "Get tae fuck, yer winding me up so you are"

2/ "I'm not at all, But here's the best bit, they made him take his turban aff. He was going radio rental"

1/ "I'm telling you that's racist in any book"

2/ "I know right! But wait to ya hear this, The eejit had a tub of six inch nails sitting on his head. Said he had no room in the box!"

1/ "Stop, I'm gonna pish masel' laughing"

2/ "I'm no joking here. It's no' funny"

1/ "No funny! Ya daft wanker it's hilarious"

2/ "Widnae be funny if he was sitting behind you, the next thing WHACK! A fucking hammer in the napper"

1/ "Ha,ha,ha Sounds like an album cover, A hammer in the napper by some Heavy Metal band hahahaha Well at least he widnae use the nine inch nails hahahahaha"

2/ "Aye by the time he got his turban aff hahahahaha"

1/ "Telt ye it wiz funny hahahahah"

2/ "Fuck, hahaha I cannae stop laughing hahahahah"

1/ "Hahahahhaha will ye forever stop hahahah"

2/ "Shame it wis'nae a popadom, I'm fucking starving hahahah"

1/ "STOP!!"

PLEASE FASTEN YOUR SEAT BELTS

1/ "Magic, must be about to land"

2/ "Happy days, Cannae wait tae get aff this plane, I'm bustin' fir a shite"

1/ "Ach, ya dirty bastard ye. Go now before the stewards tell you it's too late"

2/ "NO WAY!"

1/ "Whit? Whit is wrang wi' you? Why in the fuck not?"

2/ "I'm feart"

1/ "Eh/ Feart, feart of what?"

2/ "Ye'll laugh"

1/ "I won't"

2/ "Yer awready laughing"

1/ "Hahahaha I'll stop, See there I've stopped"

2/ "I know you ye baw bag, yer laughing now and you don't even know what at"

1/ "I'VE STOPPED! I promise"

2/ "On what?"

1/ "Whit? Whit do ya mean on what?"

2/ "What do you promise on?"

1/ "How auld are you? Right, I'll do you this If I laugh I'll gie ye twenty dollars"

2/ "Promise?"

1/ "Will you stop with aw that schoolgirl pish, I fucking promise for fucks sake"

2/ "You'll no tell naebady?"

1/ "NAW!"

2/ "Right well, You know how them bogs flush real quick an aw"

1/ "Aye, and....."

2/ "I'm feart when I flush the bog the suction will pull my arse in and I get stuck"

1/ "Hahahahahahahahahahahahahahahahahahahahahahahahahahahahah"

2/ "Ye said ye widnae laugh!"

1/ "Hahahahahahahahahahahahahhahahahahahahaha"

2/ "Yer a fucking dick splash so ye are"

1/ "Hahahahahaha ye daft cunt ye hahahahahah"

2/ "I'll batter ye wan in a minute if ye dinnae stop that pish"

1/ "Hahahah ye hahaha wipe yer hahahah stand up, oh fuck I'm gonna be sick"

2/ "GOOD YA FILTHY ROTTEN BASTARD"

1/ "Ya wipe yer arse, stand up, pull yer breeks up, put the lid down and flush hahaha Whit in the name o' fuck do you think yer sittin' on, The latest Dyson?"

2/ "WHIT?"

1/ "Aye, ye daft prick"

2/ "Hahahaha really?"

1/ "Aye hahahaha"

2/ "Fuck I've been bustin' since we left Glesga'"

1/ "Thank fuck myou've no the Tex Ritters then hahahaha"

2/ "Yer a right bassa hahahahaha"

1/ "I'm no' the fanny baws here"

2/ "Ye better no tell na wan, I'm warning ye now"

1/ "I won't hahahaha I promise hahahahah"

2/ "Stop hahahahaha fucking laughing at me hahahaha"

WE HAVE NOW LANDED IN PHILADELPHIA

"CHEESE" They both shout only to be glared at in disgust by the other passengers

2/ "Look at this, A plane fu' o' Hob Nobs"

1/ "Hahaha 'Mone let's hit the bar before the flight to Liquordale"

2/ "You'll no tell anyone now"

1/ "Naw, I promised didn't I"

Wandering off to enjoy their swallae at the bar ye can hear in the distance

"Haw Mister did I tell ye about my pal here....."

THE WEE BLACK BONNET

It's early Spring, The wee black bonnet is put away till later in
the year
In the drawer wi' his socks and those things that hold up his
rear
The wee wooly bonnet thinks I don't like it in there
So when no one's looking He nips out and off down the stair
He nips out the door and over the field
Wondering what this Summer will yield
Suddenly the wind picks up and blows him away
Landing on a branch on the old oak tree, He is stranded so
this is where he will stay
Much better than the drawer wi' his socks and those things
that hold up his rear
I wonder where I'll be this time next year
Sitting in the sun on his branch, on the tree
He becomes a nest to Mr and Mrs Birdy
They chirp, They peck but he disnae mind
For the wee black bonnet is thoughtful and kind
Autumn comes it's windy and cold

He thinks I don't want to be lonely, lonely and cold

A storm comes, lifts him up and into the air

It blows and it blows, He could land Gods know where

As chance would have it, He landed at the step

Of the house he once lived where he felt inept

He sneaks in and up the stair to the foot of drawer

He's tired and knackered and lies on the floor

"How did my wee jaggy bonnet get there on the floor"

He's put in the drawer with the socks and those things that

hold up his rear

The good news Is, It's later that year

The wee black bonnet keeps his head warm and sweaty

Did I ever tell you It was knitted by his wee auntie Betty

He'll stay in a pocket or on his head till Spring

Then It's in the drawer with his socks and those silly things.

About The Author

Originally from Prestwick in Scotland, Mark Evison has been living in Belfast for the past 10 years.

After suffering from mental health problems, Mark's counsellor suggested that he began writing. Throwing himself into the worlds of poetry and short stories, Mark shared his creations with his close friends who encouraged him to pursue publishing his first collection of poetry HOPE.

Influenced by the likes of Charles Bukowski, John Steinbeck, Seamus Heaney and Patrick Magill, Mark brings life's ordinary experiences into an exciting and innovative light.

Now, working on a journal and collection of short stories, Mark always has a story to tell. He continues to create poetry, with enough poems to fill several more collections.

Mark's first book of poetry HOPE can be purchased from: www.excaliburpress.co.uk/store/products/hope-mark-evison

Printed in Great Britain
by Amazon